A Book of One's Own

SECOND EDITION

Second Edition

A Book of One's-Own

Developing literacy through making books

Paul Johnson

Graphic illustrator: Jayne Restall

Heinemann
Portsmouth, NH

Heinemann
A division of Reed Elsevier Inc.
361 Hanover Street
Portsmouth, NH 03801-3912

Offices and agents throughout the world

First published in 1998 in Great Britain by
Hodder and Stoughton Educational
a division of Hodder Headline Plc
338 Euston Road
London NW1 3BH
GREAT BRITAIN

Copyright © 1998 Paul Johnson

Also published in the United States of America
in 1998 by Heinemann

US Cataloging-in-Publication Data is on file with the Library of Congress

Johnson, Paul, 1943–
    A book of one's own: developing literacy through making books /
Paul Johnson; graphic illustrator, Jayne Restall.
        p.   cm.
    Includes bibliographical references (p. 126).
    ISBN 0-325-00014-X
    1. Activity programs in education—Great Britain—Handbooks,
manuals, etc.   2. Book design—Great Britain—Handbooks,
manuals, etc.   3. Child authors—Great
Britain.   I. Title.
    LB1027.25.J64   1998
    372.133—dc21
                                                              98–11236
                                                              CIP

Typeset by Wearset, Boldon, Tyne and Wear
Printed in Great Britain for Hodder & Stoughton Educational, a division
of Hodder Headline Plc, 338 Euston Road, London NW1 3BH by
Redwood Books, Trowbridge, Wiltshire

Contents

3

Acknowledgements

The author would like to thank the staff and pupils of the following schools for their cooperation in the preparation of this book and allowing him to reproduce books created by them:

Beaver Road Junior School, Manchester.
Birchfields Primary School, Manchester.
Brookburn Primary School, Manchester.
Queens Road Primary School, Stockport.
Broadheath Primary School, Trafford.
Mill Hill Primary School, Oldham.
Hey with Zion Primary School, Oldham.
Sunninghill Primary School, Bolton.
Urmston Infants' School, Trafford.

A special thanks to Beryl Edwards for help in the early years field and Sian Hughes at Gateshouse Books in Manchester.

Introduction

Shortly after *A Book of One's Own* was first published in 1990 the Gulbenkian Foundation funded The Book Art Project (based at The Manchester Metropolitan University) for a two year period. The aim of the project (which was inaugurated by a Crafts Council grant in 1986) is to encourage children to develop their writing through the book form. The publication of this, my first book, together with the Gulbenkian Foundation grant enabled me to present this idea to a wider audience than had previously been possible.

What was particularly attractive to teachers and parents was that most of the book forms suggested in *A Book of One's Own* and subsequently in *Literacy Through the Book Arts* (1993), and *Books Searching for Authors* (1994), could be constructed from single sheets of paper. Many of these books require scissors as the only piece of equipment necessary to make them. Only when sections are cut from *inside* a sheet is a craft knife necessary. Consequently a whole class of children can make them easily and simultaneously.

I could not have imagined in 1990 that over the next few years invitations would come from all over the country and beyond – from Italy, Austria, The Netherlands, Fiji, The Solomon Islands and the USA – for me to run courses for parents and teachers in how to make these books, and how writing could be conceived inside them. Letters come to me daily from around the world which speak of the influence of these books on promoting self-assurance and a sense of achievement in the young when other approaches to communicating on paper have failed. Interest has also come from those working amongst long-stay patients in hospitals (books that can be made in the hand are perfect for someone who is immobile) and a group of East Midlands parents have written to me saying how much these book forms have influenced the strategies they use for teaching their children at home.

As I researched the role of the book arts in education it became evident that making books was not only pleasurable and fulfilling for children, but that it helped them to think and plan what they wanted to say in words and pictures. This element is as relevant to non-fiction as to story writing. In the basic origami book (see page 20) the author is required to organise his or her material into six pages. Whether one is engaged on writing about how to bake a cake, describing the highlights of a holiday, or examining the rain cycle the pupils are conditioned to think in a 'page way' just like professional authors. No other means of writing is quite so successful at this as the book arts!

In revising *A Book of One's Own* I was conscious that its popularity sprung essentially from the book forms it described. For this reason I have replaced some of the original text with new book ideas. Some of them have come from the American paper artist, Edward Hutchins. We started to correspond after becoming aware of each other's work and now a steady exchange of ideas cross the Atlantic. Another consideration when revising this book came from the difficulty some found in interpreting the working diagrams. There is no substitute for being shown in person how to do something; graphic representation is second best. However, I hope that the more complex book forms are easier to follow in this revised edition.

New to this revised edition is the setting of book art in a multicultural context, and consideration of special needs aspects of the genre. I have also provided a section on publishing in the classroom – an area that has gained impetus since I wrote the original book.

People often ask me if I have invented all these books forms. Unfortunately, I am unable to seek a patent on any of them. What a sense of satisfaction I would have felt if I had invented the simple origami book! Eclectically, I have taken ideas from traditional Japanese paper folding and combined them with the innovations of the great nineteenth century German paper engineer, Lothar Meggendorfer. One book found its genesis in a 3-D advertisement in my local building society, and a novel way of folding a table napkin by a restaurant I ate in has been used as the base for more than one book. Everywhere I go I say: please let me have any new book form ideas you come up with. I say the same here. But the book form is meaningless without serious attention given to *what goes inside it*. I cannot stress too forcefully that both technical paper form and written and illustrated content must be seen as one related process. Only then can the book be experienced as a total organism conveying clearly expressed ideas through the magic and wonder of folded paper.

1 Story making for story books

There have been many arguments for and against the use of the narrative genre in teaching children to write. My own view is that narrative writing embraces so many genres of writing – argument and discussion can feature in stories as well as description and letter writing, and besides, it is part of the child's inheritance and does so much to cultivate imaginative vision. However, it does not follow that the young always find the craft of story writing easy. The imagination does not always behave in a structured way and worst of all, it may fail to function or at least seem paralysed. How many children chew their pencils in class because they can't think what to write? Here are some of the techniques I use to 'release' stories from children and get some kind of structure in the process.

Unlocking the imagination

The rusty door – This most common kind of door is fastened by misuse. But being too insistent on a creative response can be counter-productive: ('Now I want us to think out all the furnishings inside the castle. John, you tell us about the pictures on the walls, and Mary, you tell us what is on the mantelpiece . . .') Children can be frightened by not being able to 'think of something'. Most destructive of all is to tell the class what an unimaginative lot they all are. Children must feel at ease with you, the story conductor. The orchestral conductor does not make the music him or her self but draws music out of the players. A regular story improvisation can do much to facilitate the opening of the imagination's door. The daily 'diary' of the early years classroom in which pupils describe the previous day's events and the next day's expectations is a good preparation for inventing stories. Lazy pupils need prodding and the introverted need coaxing. Of course one must be cautious: quiet or non-communicative children may find it easier to express themselves in writing than talk aloud, and active verbalisers may find difficulty in writing clearly what they have found so easy to say.

The well-oiled door – In nearly every class there is at least one child who is 'good' at telling or creating stories. If you have one of these godsends use him or her as an associate conductor when improvised stories dry up. Another door is marked **Popular Imagery**. To ask for a character to start a story improvisation can elicit something like Donald Duck or a pop star. Larger than life characters have less story potential than a boy called Alex or a lady called Mrs Thompson. Stereotypes have to be replaced with simple yet convincing images that can be worked on. In an improvisation one might say, 'Well, yes, the president of the USA was there, but who else?'

A door marked **Common Place Imagery** attracts settings like the classroom the pupils are in or a supermarket. There is nothing wrong with these providing they can be seen in a less familiar light, like a noise coming from a classroom cupboard or a supermarket full of magic sauce bottles. Sometimes when accepting a commonplace, say a milkman, I endeavour to winkle out of the class a detailed description of his appearance with asides like – 'Why does he walk with a limp?' The door marked **Personal Images** reveals characters or situations from stories currently being read by pupils. Is the offered character from the child's imagination or 'lifted' from a book or TV series? Of course story characters can be written about and given new roles to play, but as story conductor one must try to help them have a life of their own.

Somehow every pupil should be involved in making stories however small or insignificant their role. One makes suggestions where necessary, 'stands back' when the story is flowing, injects new ideas when the plot is flagging. The greatest gift a story conductor can bestow is the illusion that the class is making the whole story themselves – that you are an observer not an active creator yourself. Only then will the whole story seem theirs.

Children grow weary easily and have a low threshold of boredom. Timing is therefore crucial to success. So is body language and facial gesture. One can bring alive a character by emphasising the inflections of spoken dialogue, dialect or vocal dynamics: '. . . and in the field was a box and when Sarah got CLOSE TO IT WHAT SHOULD **SHE FIND BUT** . . .'

Making up a story is one thing but turning it into a story book is something else. A description of a book making project with a class of eight year-olds suggests just one way to go about it.

Stories from boxes
From my top pocket I produced a small box-like object. I proceeded to speculate with the class who could have owned it and what it could be used for, before telling them that it was a prayer wheel I had brought back from Darjeeling many years before. We then made up a whole new story about it.

Drafting and presenting
Working in rough books I invited the class to begin again with the box idea but this time to make their own story. As their stories grew they were shared with other pupils, edited and revised and then it was time to transfer them to the concertina book form. It is the simplest book to make and so the most adaptable. In this variation of the form a cover panel is attached to the front of two folded page spreads. Through a window cut in this cover the viewer sees a drawing of the box drawn on the back of the first page. The main episodes into which their stories fell had to be transposed to the folds of the book. We looked at examples of professional writers and illustrators working together and discussed how the story 'fitted' the page.

① NAME CHARACTER. HE/SHE GOES SOMEWHERE

② SOMETHING INTERESTING HAPPENS TO HIM/HER

③ WHAT INTERESTING THING HAPPENS NEXT?

HOW DOES THE STORY FINISH?

DO YOU WANT HALF OR FULL PAGE TEXT?

OR DO YOU WANT TO TRY ANOTHER ARRANGEMENT?

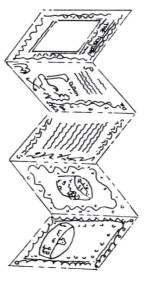

Parts of the story had to be selected for visual presentation. Which events or situations were the most interesting? Should a picture accompany the text? Where on the page should the picture go? To help this process page layout suggestions were drawn on the board and pupils selected or invented their own arrangements.

In Andrea's story a lady finds a box on a supermarket shelf. Inside the box is another box and inside that box is a beautiful girl . . .

Continuous concertina book

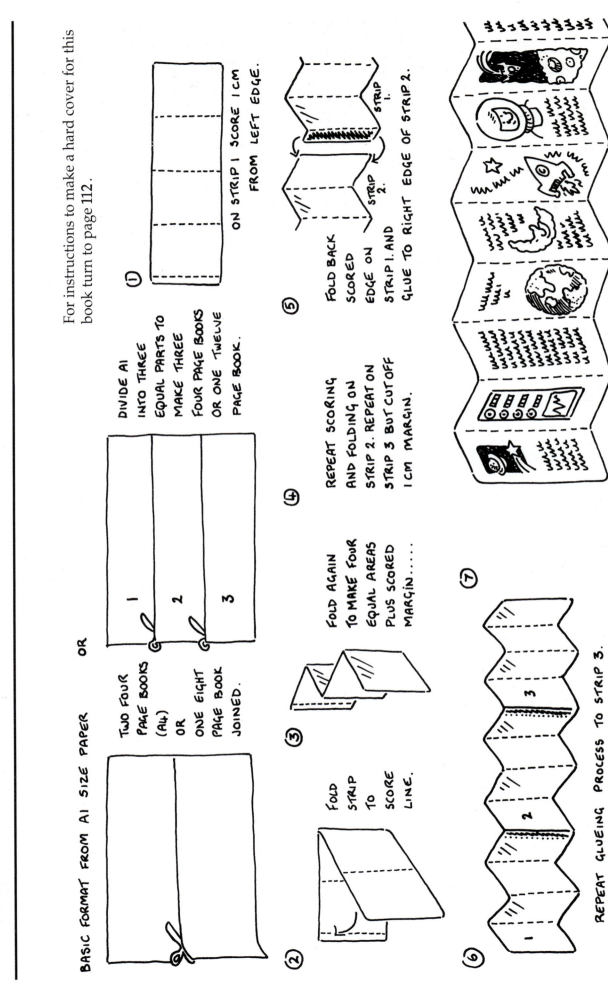

For instructions to make a hard cover for this book turn to page 112.

BASIC FORMAT FROM A1 SIZE PAPER   OR

TWO FOUR PAGE BOOKS (A4) OR ONE EIGHT PAGE BOOK JOINED.

DIVIDE A1 INTO THREE EQUAL PARTS TO MAKE THREE FOUR PAGE BOOKS OR ONE TWELVE PAGE BOOK.

① ON STRIP 1 SCORE 1CM FROM LEFT EDGE.

② FOLD STRIP TO SCORE LINE.

③ FOLD AGAIN TO MAKE FOUR EQUAL AREAS PLUS SCORED MARGIN......

④ REPEAT SCORING AND FOLDING ON STRIP 2. REPEAT ON STRIP 3 BUT CUT OFF 1CM MARGIN.

⑤ FOLD BACK SCORED EDGE ON STRIP 1. AND GLUE TO RIGHT EDGE OF STRIP 2.

⑥

⑦ REPEAT GLUEING PROCESS TO STRIP 3.

9

Eight page concertina book

This concertina book is made by following the folding pattern to make eight rectangles described on page 61. When the book is folded down there are a maximum of seven pages to write on and a 'cover' page. The page before last can be the last page of the story or project, or used to give details about the author or a synopsis of the story. The illustration shows the book in its opened-up format.

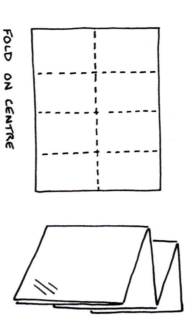

FOLD ON CENTRE HORIZONTALLY AND THEN CONCERTINA INTO FOUR PAGES.

On the first page of Lee's book he describes all the excitement of being somewhere new. The next page contrasts this with an illustration of him having his breakfast. It is captioned as one might a photograph album. Next is a combined text and illustration page sketching a day out 'taking pictures', and the last page completes the book with a line drawing of the photograph Lee has taken of the night sky before returning home. The rear side of the concertina holds the cover, and on the far page a drawing of the holiday cottage.

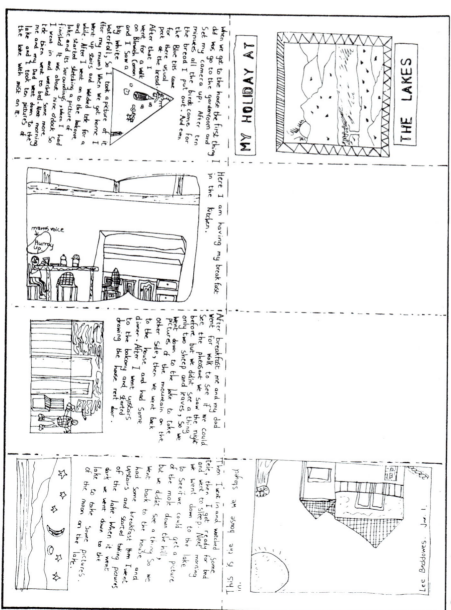

My holiday at the Lakes by Lee (7)

② Books from one sheet of paper

It is open to debate at what stage a folded birthday-type card can be described as a leaflet, a booklet, or a booklet a book. Necessity breeds invention so that which is to be communicated should determine, to some extent at least, the format of the publication. A short poem, depiction or reflection fits neatly into the single fold of the greeting card. An adventure story asks for something more ambitious. Professional graphic designers arrange the copy (words) given to them by a

client and accompanying artwork into the constraints of paper size and folded divisions required to fit, for example, things like a standard envelope. Above all, pupils are faced with the challenge of where to place both words and images successfully so they both communicate clearly and look 'good'. The book and book-like forms which follow take the single fold as the point at which a book can take shape. Without a fold we have a poster or single sheet handout. From here

endless creative inventions are possible. The golden rule of the Japanese paper folding genre is that nothing is added and nothing taken away from the sheet. I have tried to follow that discipline. It also brings with it other advantages: for example, there is no waste, pages cannot be lost, and cutting multiple book forms (see page 123) is relatively easy. See folding instructions on page 61.

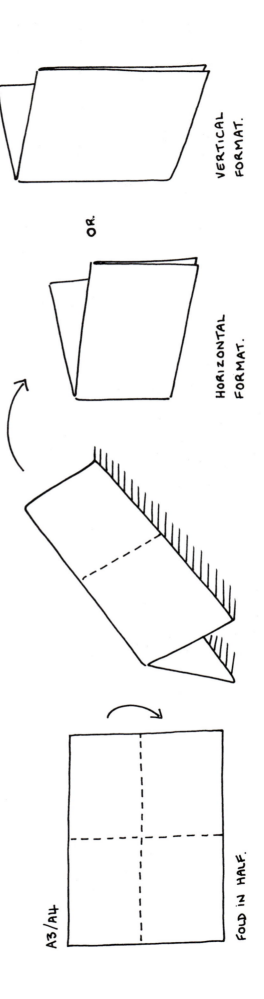

VERTICAL FORMAT.

OR.

HORIZONTAL FORMAT.

FOLD IN HALF.

A3/A4

Folded card with door

An added advantage to the double page is that doors and windows can be cut to provide stimulus for thematic story development. The *Music Soldier* by Daniel (5) shows this to good effect, as does the same strategy in developed form, *The Castle House* by Jennifer (6).

'The Castle House' by Jennifer (6) Door closed . . . Door open . . .

'The Music Soldier' by Daniel (5)

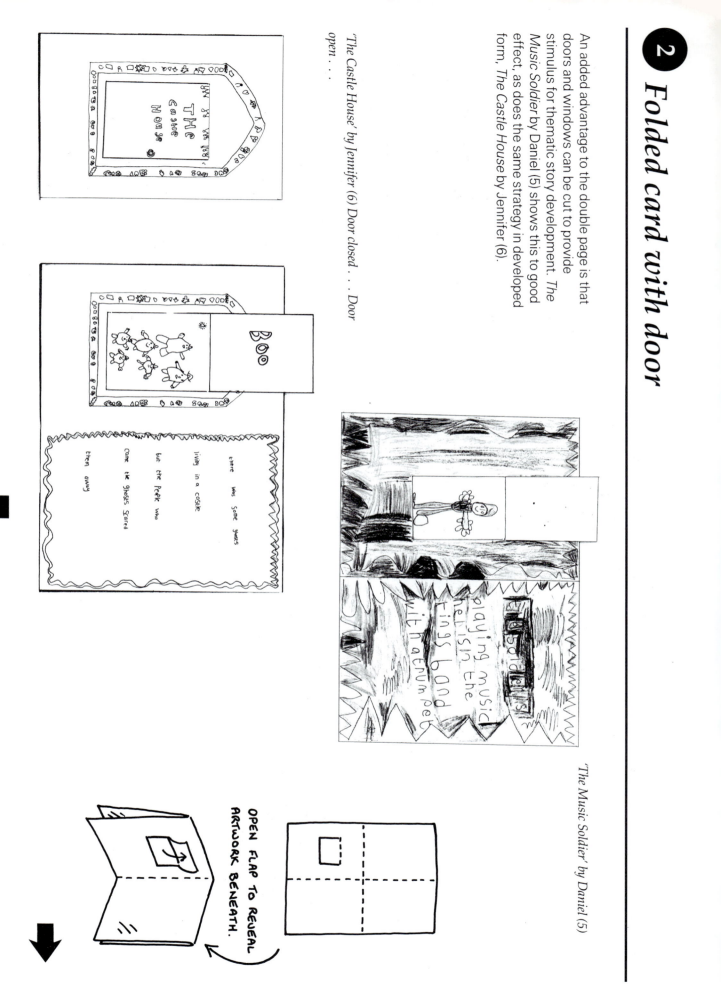

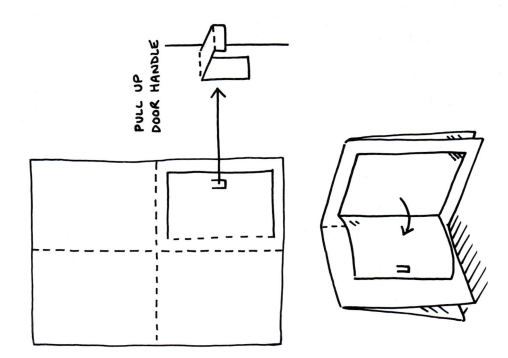

'The Monster' by John (8)

The Monster by John (8) intensifies the door theme by cutting a pull-up door handle. The quality of John's artwork has been stimulated by the novelty of the folded presentation.

This design stimulates a single folded story which is hidden and therefore thematically secret, private or in Andrew's case, ghostly. To augment the mood of ghostliness everything is back to front; the booklet opens from right to left and all the writing inside is from right to left too!

① FOLD A3 AS SHOWN. ON BOTTOM RIGHT PANEL CUT DOOR WITH CORRESPONDING LEFT PANEL SLOT.

② FOLD TO A5. FOLD DOOR FLAP AROUND .....

③ AND LOCK INTO SLOT ON REVERSE.

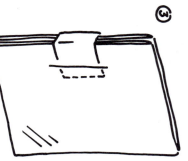

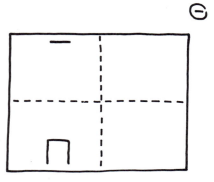

'Ghost Hunter Secret File' by Andrew (8)

① A3 VERTICAL FORMAT. CUT OUT WINDOW IN BOTTOM RIGHT PANEL.

②

FOLD TO A4 THEN TO A5

③

CUTTING PLAN

④

DRAW THROUGH A 1 CM MARGIN TO THE FOLDED SHEET BENEATH AND CUT OUT TO MAKE MOUNT FOR ARTWORK INSIDE CARD.

Cover

Inside card

This method of presentation produces a double mounted piece of artwork supported by writing. Moira (9) made a white line on coloured background illustration of a small trinket box in the shape of a duck. This was made by inscribing the design with a hard pencil (HB, 1H) through tracing paper to cartridge beneath. This makes a light incision in the cartridge which can be crayoned over to produce the unique white line effect shown. The finished artwork was glued into the picture area, the story written to accompany it and a title incorporated into the cover design. Finally, a decorative border was applied to the mounted area.

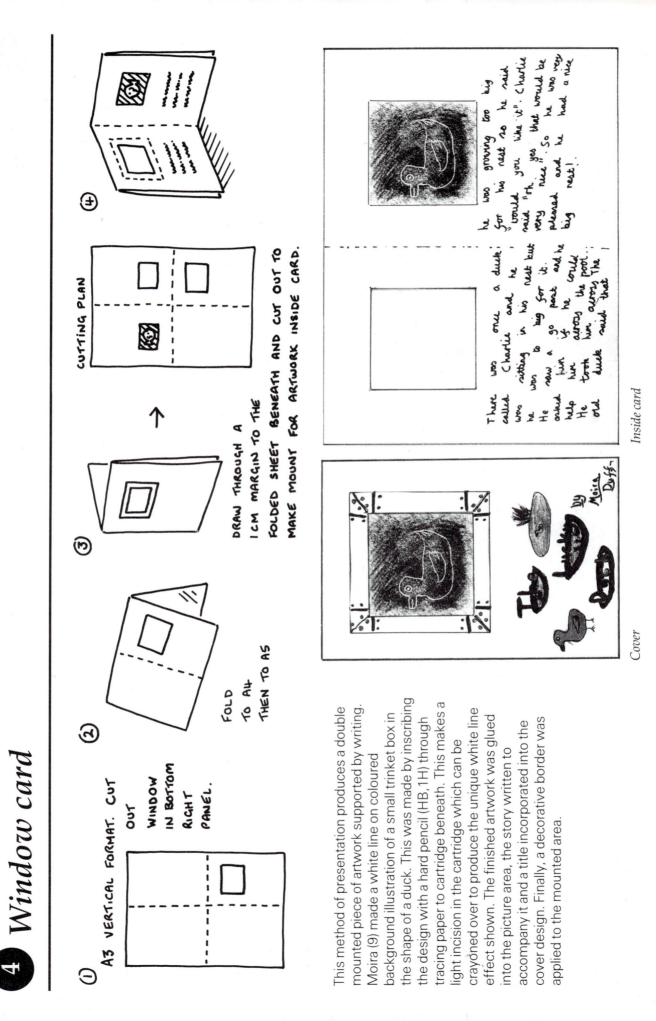

Presentation card

This is an attractive locked card suitable for invitations and celebrations.

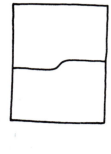

①

A4

FOLD ON HORIZONTAL.

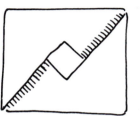

② MAKE LOOP OF STRIP, ENSURING THAT FOLDS ARE AVOIDED.

③ CUT "V" SLOT THROUGH THE FOUR SHEETS.

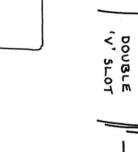

VARIATIONS :-

DOUBLE 'V' SLOT

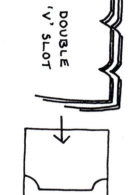
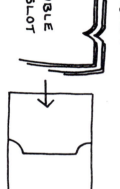

④ OPEN STRIP AND LOCK INTO CYLINDER

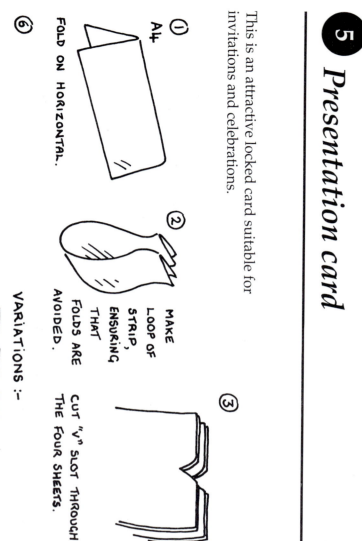

⑤ WITH LOCK IN THE CENTRE PRESS CYLINDER FLAT TO FORM CARD.

⑥

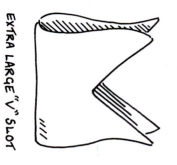

EXTRA LARGE "V" SLOT

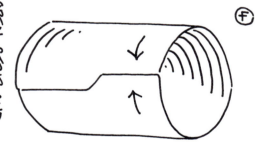

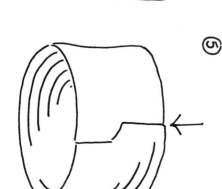

Invitation card designed by Stuart (8).

6 Haiku poem fold and origami envelope

Before moving on to the next stage of basic books, I want to include a very intimate interrelationship of two sheets of A4 paper. The simplicity of beauty is so inspiringly manifested in the Haiku poem (lines of 5,7,5 syllables) and what could be more appropriate than a simple origami envelope to hold the words?

John (9) wrote:

'When the day is gone
The moon and stars shine brightly
And dreams fill the world.'

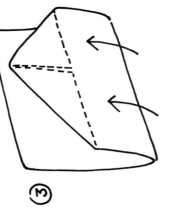

①

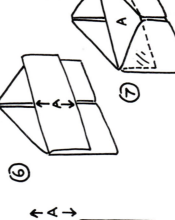

③

②

FOLD CORNERS TO CENTRE.

LIFT BASE AND FOLD TO A5.

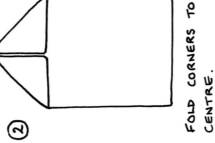

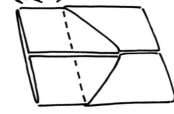

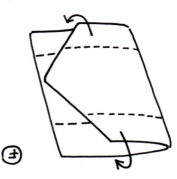

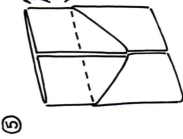

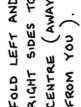

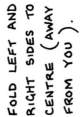

⑤

⑥

⑦ A

TURN OVER.

FOLD 'A' DOWN AND TUCK INTO FLAPS.

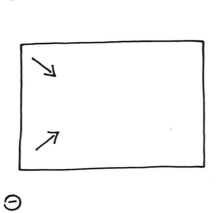

④

FOLD LEFT AND RIGHT SIDES TO CENTRE (AWAY FROM YOU).

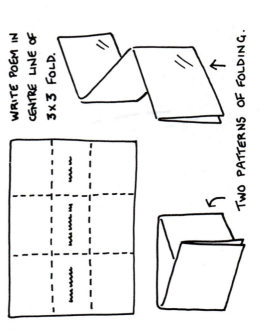

WRITE POEM IN CENTRE LINE OF 3x3 FOLD.

TWO PATTERNS OF FOLDING.

Tabernacle card

Here two 'doors' of equal proportion enclose a back panel with vaulted roof.

① A4 HORIZONTAL

FOLD OUTER EDGES TO CENTRE. TO FIND CENTRE WITHOUT CREASING PAPER MAKE A LOOP. MARK HALFWAY POINT ALONG TOP EDGE WITH FINGERNAIL 'X'.

② [arrows pointing to X]

③ FOLD CORNERS TO CENTRE

④ FOLD CORNERS BACK AND PUSH INWARDS

When laid top-down, Kate (8) thought that the form looked like a frog. This stimulated frog artwork on the outside central panel, and a story 'The Ferocious Frog' on the outside (door) panels.

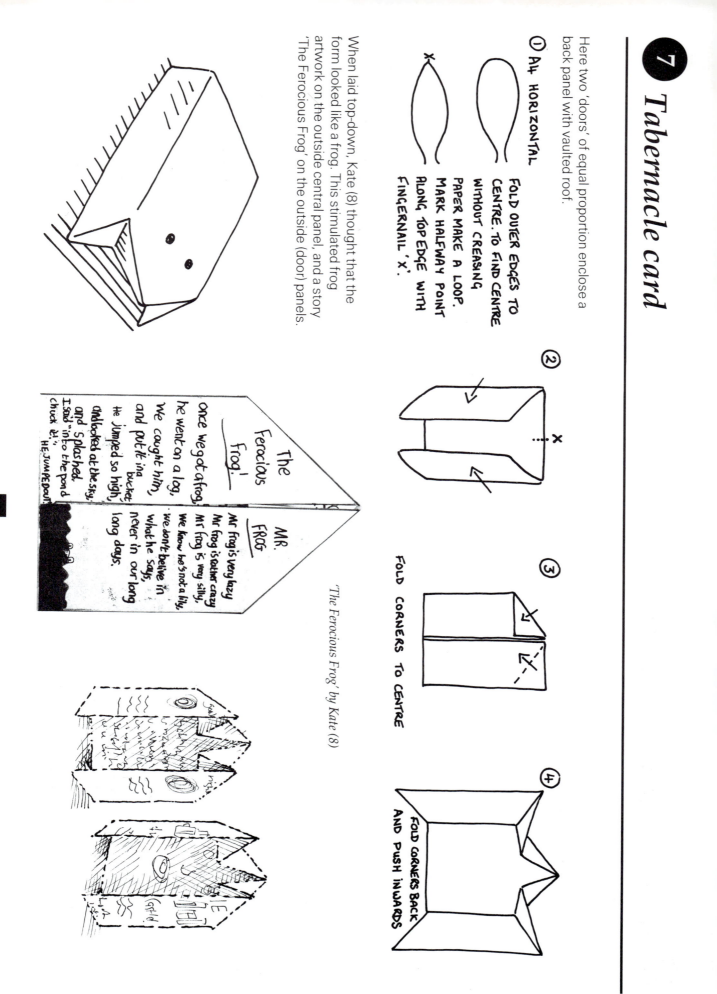

The Ferocious Frog!

Once we got a frog. he went on a log. we caught him, and put it in a bucket. he jumped so high, and looked at the sky, and splashed. I said "into the pond chuck it". HE JUMPED OUT.

MR. FROG.

Mr frog is very lazy. Mr frog is rather crazy. Mr frog is very silly, we know he's not a lily. we don't belive in what he says, never in our long long days.

'The Ferocious Frog' by Kate (8)

8 Irregular concertina book

Sarah (8) invented this one – 'The Magic Tree Seed' – a series of concertina folds which increase in size. Her story, about a growing tree, prompted the book's invention, so that 'the book could grow like a tree'.

'The Magic Tree Seed' by Sarah (8)

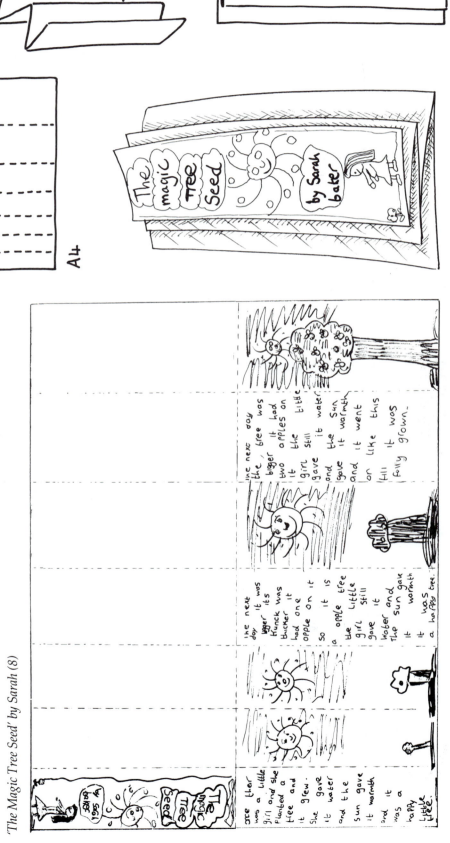

FOLD ON HORIZONTAL.

A4

The simplicity of this book makes it immediately accessible for large-class production whilst being more novel than a simple folded concertina. If children are capable of using scissors, they can make the whole book themselves. I must have seen several hundred origami books by children, on every conceivable theme from stories to recipes, local studies to illustrated journals.

'My Best Friend' by Lisa (6)

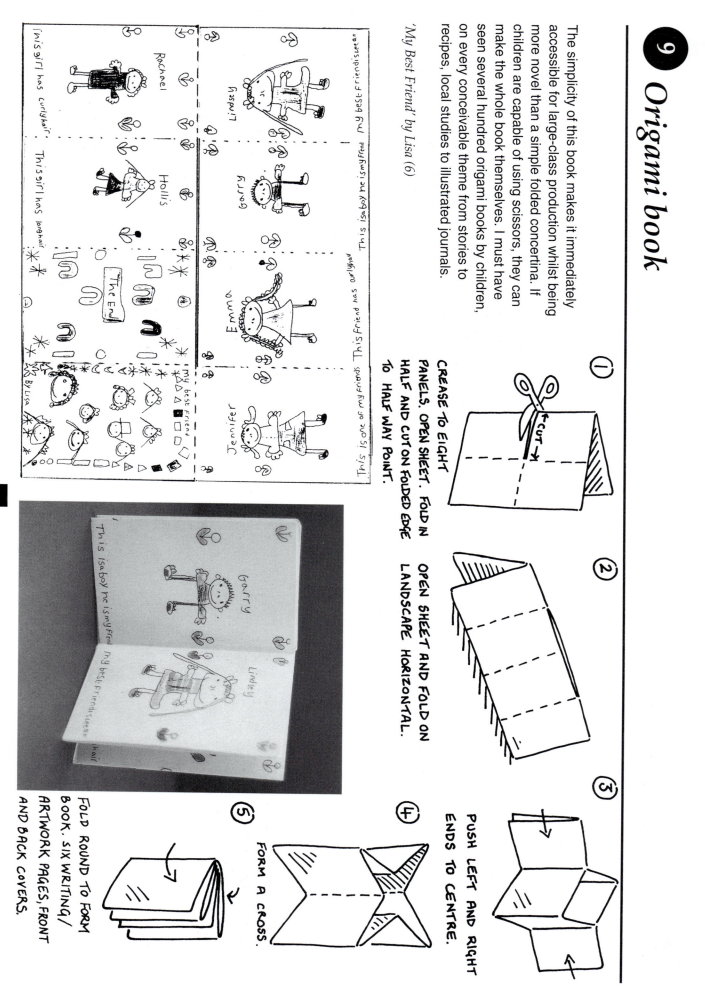

① CREASE TO EIGHT PANELS. OPEN SHEET. FOLD IN HALF AND CUT ON FOLDED EDGE TO HALF WAY POINT.

② OPEN SHEET AND FOLD ON LANDSCAPE HORIZONTAL.

③ PUSH LEFT AND RIGHT ENDS TO CENTRE.

④ FORM A CROSS.

⑤ FOLD ROUND TO FORM BOOK. SIX WRITING/ ARTWORK PAGES, FRONT AND BACK COVERS.

20

 **Origami House book**

One of the fascinating things about the origami book is that it can be presented as a three-dimensional form. Leo's *Flying House*, a variation of the origami house book, is displayed like an architect's model. If wished, the inside of the building can be drawn too. The building can be conceived as 'My House' or 'The Magic House' with the narrative written on the side panels. In a geographical context the theme could be 'Houses in Other Parts of the World' and in a religious studies context mosques, synagogues and churches can be made in a similar way.

Flying house by Leo (6)

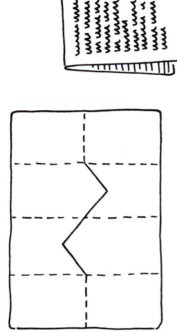

CREASE SHEET VERTICALLY IN HALF AND HALF AGAIN IN THE SAME DIRECTION. OPEN SHEET. DRAW A LINE THROUGH THE CENTRE AND CUT PANELS AS SHOWN.

FOLLOW DIAGRAMS 2 AND 3 FROM 'ORIGAMI' BOOK.

21

Other origami variations

Other variations of the three-dimensional origami book include this castle which could make a history project more realistic. By cutting side panels and doors the basic castle can be made more complex.

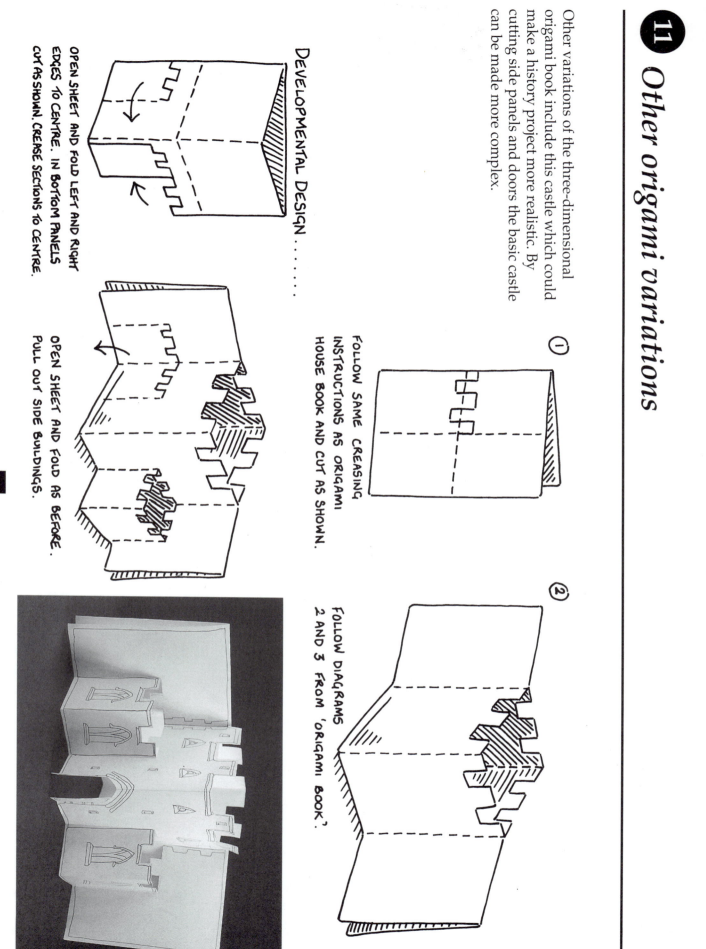

DEVELOPMENTAL DESIGN . . . .

OPEN SHEET AND FOLD LEFT AND RIGHT EDGES TO CENTRE. IN BOTTOM PANELS CUT AS SHOWN, CREASE SECTIONS TO CENTRE.

OPEN SHEET AND FOLD AS BEFORE. PULL OUT SIDE BUILDINGS.

① FOLLOW SAME CREASING INSTRUCTIONS AS ORIGAMI HOUSE BOOK AND CUT AS SHOWN.

② FOLLOW DIAGRAMS 2 AND 3 FROM 'ORIGAMI BOOK'.

⑫ Triangle book

Story and pictures in 3 triangular sequences . . . .

One of the conventions of basic, one-sheet books is that the pages tend to be of the A5 format. A way of arriving at a different shape book 'from an A2 base is as follows:

①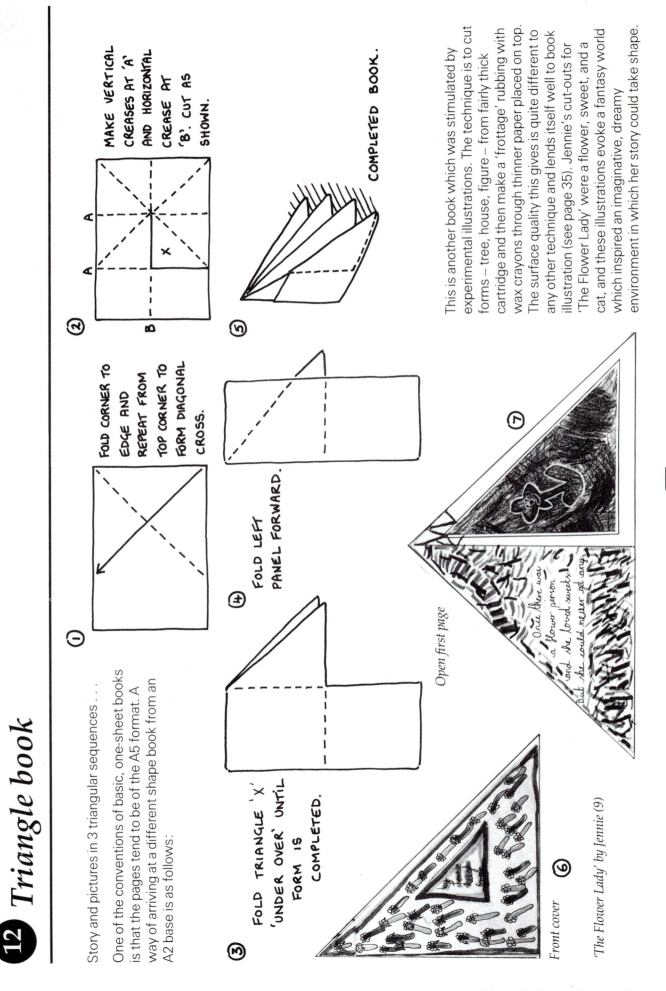

FOLD CORNER TO EDGE AND REPEAT FROM TOP CORNER TO FORM DIAGONAL CROSS.

② MAKE VERTICAL CREASES AT 'A' AND HORIZONTAL CREASE AT 'B'. CUT AS SHOWN.

⑤ COMPLETED BOOK.

④ FOLD LEFT PANEL FORWARD.

③ FOLD TRIANGLE 'X' 'UNDER OVER' UNTIL FORM IS COMPLETED.

Open first page

Front cover ⑥

⑦

'The Flower Lady' by Jennie (9)

This is another book which was stimulated by experimental illustrations. The technique is to cut forms – tree, house, figure – from fairly thick cartridge and then make a 'frottage' rubbing with wax crayons through thinner paper placed on top. The surface quality this gives is quite different to any other technique and lends itself well to book illustration (see page 35). Jennie's cut-outs for 'The Flower Lady' were a flower, sweet, and a cat, and these illustrations evoke a fantasy world which inspired an imaginative, dreamy environment in which her story could take shape.

23

Books with doors

One of the most popular single sheet books with children is described next. A conventional four-fold concertina book is made from horizontally folded A2, but instead of leaving the pages blank, hinged openings are cut into the four folds. This approach has already been discussed, but here I show a more developed way of working.

'Blast Off by Matthew and Davydd (10) (openings closed)

A2

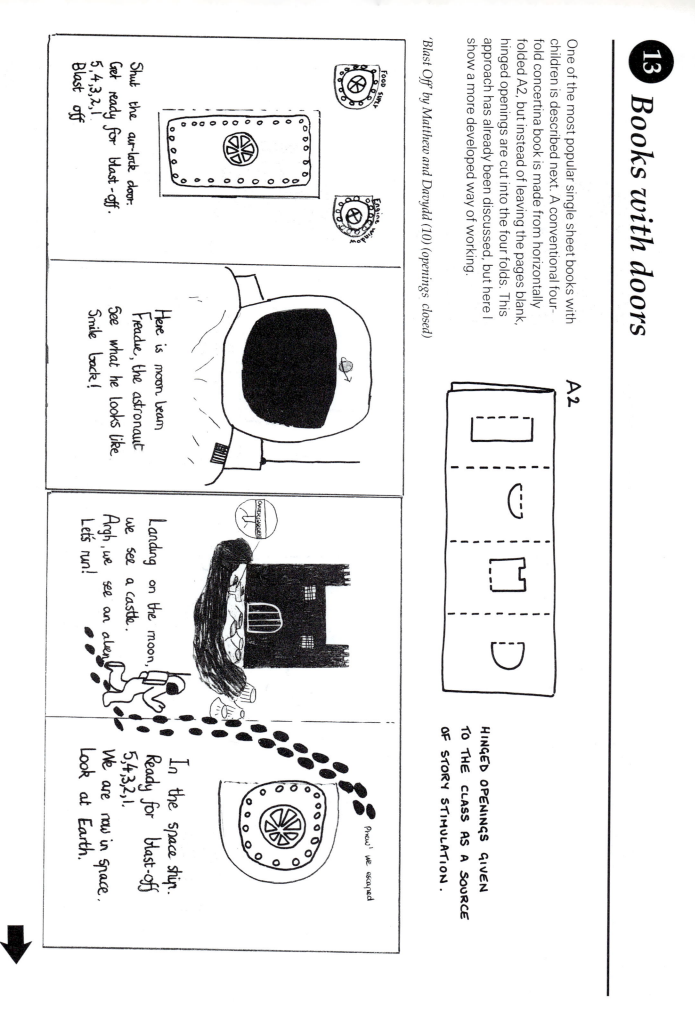

HINGED OPENINGS GIVEN
TO THE CLASS AS A SOURCE
OF STORY STIMULATION.

FOOD SUPPLY

Engine window

Shut the air-lock door.
Get ready for blast-off.
5, 4, 3, 2, 1.
Blast off

Here is moon beam
Freddie, the astronaut.
See what he looks like.
Smile back!

CANTER GARDEN

Landing on the moon,
we see a castle.
Argh, we see an alien.
Let's run!

Phew! we escaped

In the space ship.
Ready for blast-off.
5, 4, 3, 2, 1.
We are now in space.
Look at Earth.

Cover design

Experiment by cutting folded doors, windows and openings into the bottom panels as shown. An added challenge is to cut shapes in a free, unpreconceived way. The task is then to give meaning to them in story form. This form of presentation is exemplified by two groups using the same shaped openings. What is fascinating is the contrasting imagery derived from them (see next page). The dedication to design, layout, handwriting and story illustrates just how powerful an incentive an imaginatively prepared challenge is to children.

Openings open

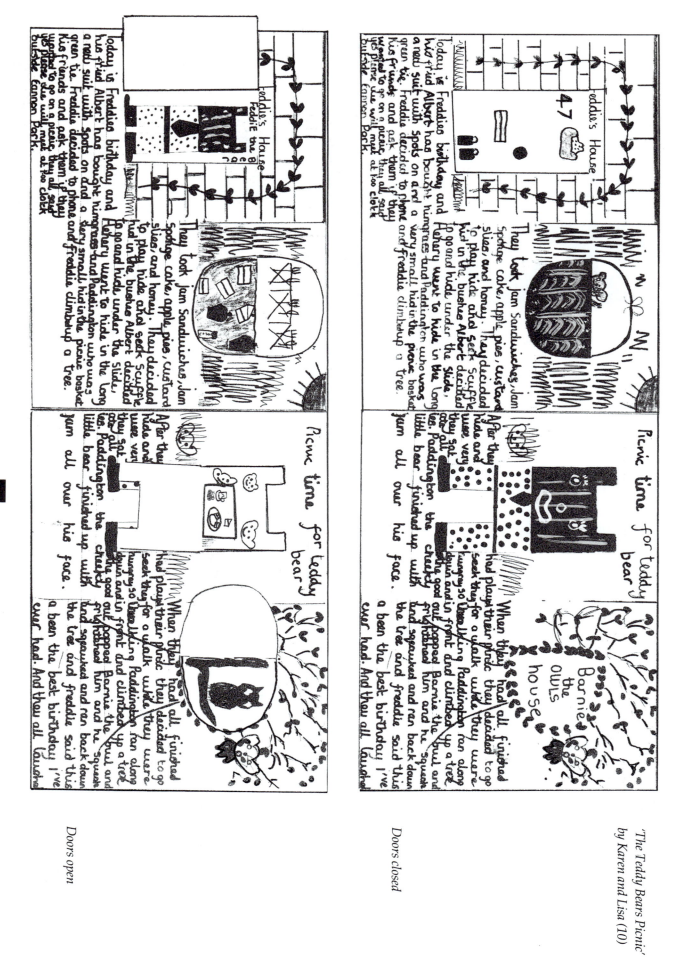

Freddie's House

47

Today is Freddies birthday and his friad Albert has bought humphres and Paddington who was a new suit with spots on and a very small hid in the picnic basket green tie. Freddie decided to phone and Freddie climbed up a tree. his friends and ask them if they wanted to go on a picnic they all said yes please she will meet at too clock outside cannon Park.

Freddie's House
Freddie the Bear

Today is Freddies birthday and his friad Albert has bought humphres and Paddington who was a new suit with spots on and a very small hid in the picnic basket green tie. Freddie decided to phone and Freddie climbed up a tree. his friends and ask them if they wanted to go on a picnic they all said yes please the will meet at too clock outside cannon Park.

They took jam Sandwiches, jam sponge cake, apple, pies, custard slice, and honey. They decided to play hide and seek Scuffle hid in the bushes Albert decided to go and hide under the slide, Flahary went to hide in the Longie. Paddington the cheeky little bear finished up with jam all over his face.

They took jam Sandwiches, jam sponge cake, apple, pies, custard slice, and honey. They decided to play hide and seek Scuffle hid in the bushes Albert decided to go and hide under the slide, Flahary went to hide in the Longie. Paddington the cheeky little bear finished up with jam all over his face.

Picnic time for teddy bear

Barnie the owls house

When they had all finished had played their picnic they decided to go seek they for a walk while they were hungry so then liking Paddington ran along cold again and in front and climbed up a tree. Paddington the cheeky good out papoad Barnie the owl and frightened him and he squeaked and ran back down the tree and freddie said this a been the best birthday I've ever had. And they all laughed.

Picnic time for teddy bear

After they had played their picnic they decided to go seek they for a walk while they were hungry so then liking Paddington ran along again and in front and climbed up a tree. When they had all finished the good out papoad Barnie the cheaky little bear finished up with jam all over his face. frightened him and he squeak and squeaked and run back down the tree and freddie said this a been the best birthday I've ever had. And they all laughed.

Doors open

Doors closed

'The Teddy Bears Picnic'
by Karen and Lisa (10)

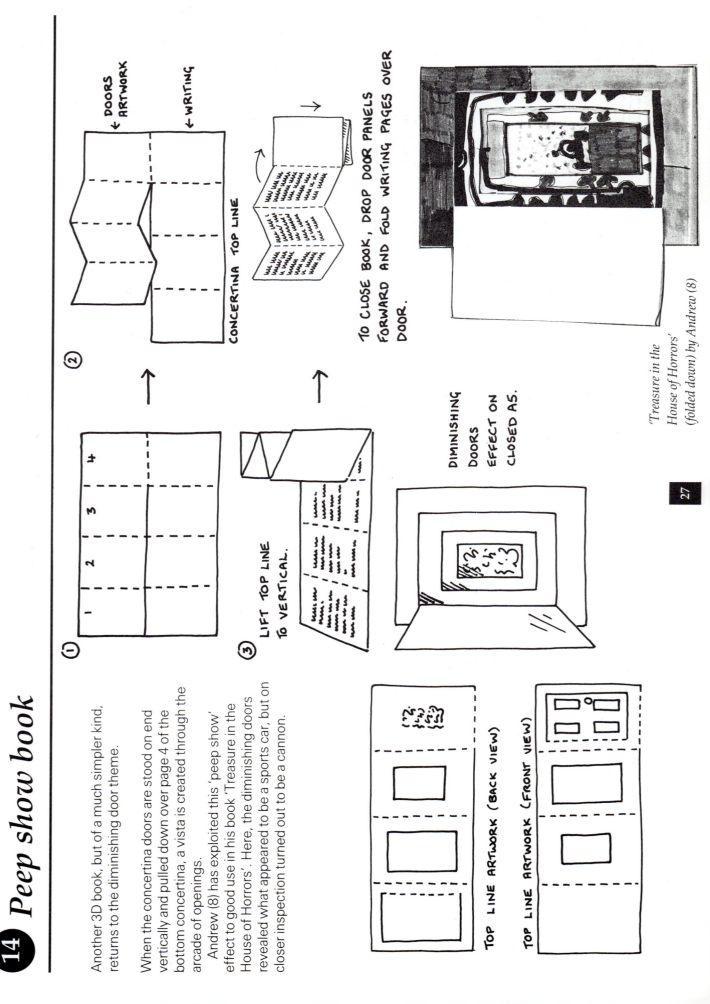

⑭ Peep show book

Another 3D book, but of a much simpler kind, returns to the diminishing door theme.

When the concertina doors are stood on end vertically and pulled down over page 4 of the bottom concertina, a vista is created through the arcade of openings.

Andrew (8) has exploited this 'peep show' effect to good use in his book 'Treasure in the House of Horrors'. Here, the diminishing doors revealed what appeared to be a sports car, but on closer inspection turned out to be a cannon.

① 1 2 3 4

② ← DOORS ARTWORK
← WRITING

CONCERTINA TOP LINE

③ LIFT TOP LINE TO VERTICAL.

To CLOSE BOOK, DROP DOOR PANELS FORWARD AND FOLD WRITING PAGES OVER DOOR.

DIMINISHING DOORS EFFECT ON CLOSED AS.

TOP LINE ARTWORK (BACK VIEW)

TOP LINE ARTWORK (FRONT VIEW)

'Treasure in the House of Horrors' (folded down) by Andrew (8)

The opening 'door and window'-style book can be engineered as a single page presentation. I am indebted to Janet, one of my BEd students, for this invention.

Although the prospect of cutting so many apertures is a daunting proposition, using the multiple cutting technique quickens the process of manufacture for a whole class. A simpler approach would be to reduce the number of openings.

This is possibly the most complex of the books suggested here, although the cutting and folding procedure is really quite simple. In Matthew's book, he traces a journey into Dracula's wardrobe to the glass where he keeps his false teeth!

FOLD A2 TO A5s

DRAW DOOR ON FRONT OF BOOK, OPEN OUT AND CUT.
FOLD DOWN AGAIN TO A5. OPEN DOOR AND DRAW
THROUGH No 2 DOOR.
REPEAT PROCESS TO DOOR No 7.

④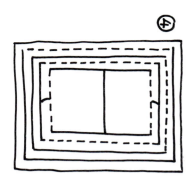

⑤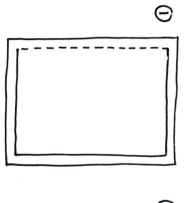

⑥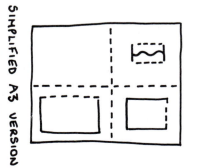

⑦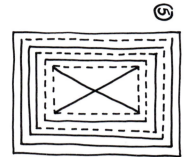

①

②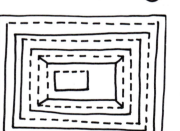

③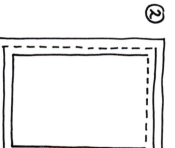

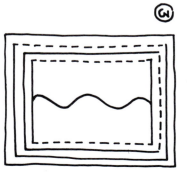

SIMPLIFIED A3 VERSION
USING 3 DOORS.